A Venture Capital Handbook:
Best Practice Strategies for Investing in Microalgae Biodiesel

Dr. David A. Blum

ISBN:0692258353
ISBN-13:9780692258354

DEDICATION

This book is dedicated to the successful exists for
all independent venture capitalists.

CONTENTS

ACKNOWLEDGMENTS

A special thanks to my editor who encouraged this project and helped along the way. In addition, I would like to thank the venture capitalists who made themselves available to answer discuss issues regarding microalgae biodiesel.

INTRODUCTION

As an independent venture capitalist (IVC), have you considered investing in the algae biodiesel? Are you unsure what algae biodiesel is? Do you want to learn some best practice strategies when investing in algae biodiesel portfolio firms? If the answer is yes, then this handbook is for you.

IVC firms invest under the pressure of various uncertainties, which influence IVC renewable energy decision-making from early stages through late funding stages. In order to reduce uncertainties, directors and managers at IVC firms need to utilize two fundamental best practice strategies: the returns model and due diligence. In addition, IVCs must understand four macro areas of uncertainty when investing in renewable energy solutions such as algae biodiesel.

The U.S. economy requires reliable and in-expensive sources of energy to fuel economic growth and create wealth. The need to locate reliable, abundant, and sustainable sources of energy is critical to the nation's economic, social, and environmental development.

The term *biofuels* refers to renewable fuels from biological sources that can be used for heat, electricity, and fuel. Biofuels could play an essential role in replacing petroleum as a viable alternative toward reducing long-term carbon dioxide (CO_2) emissions. Biodiesel, in general, is considered a promising sustainable source of energy to replace petrol diesel while meeting existing and future transportation fuel needs of the United States. However, the transition from fossil fuel use to biodiesel requires significant amounts of funding.

Experts suggest biodiesel derived from algae is the sole sustainable and abundant transportation fuel source that can replace petrol diesel. Scientists at National Renewable Energy Laboratory in Golden, Colorado; Oak Ridge National Laboratory in Oak Ridge, Tennessee; Pacific Northwest National Laboratory in Richland, Washington; and Sandia National Laboratories in Albuquerque, New Mexico are working to make algae biodiesel cost efficient and scalable.

To acquire funding, algae biodiesel producers need to collaborate with IVC firms. IVC firms are considered to be the leading source of entrepreneurial early stage equity funding for high technology business ventures. However, only 1/6 of 1% of portfolio companies meet the specific IVC firm funding requirements. Of those firms receiving venture funding less than twenty percent survive to a successful exit in terms of an initial public offering, sales, acquisition, or merger.

When funding a biodiesel portfolio firm the development and production of biodiesel is fraught with economic uncertainties similar to other technological investments. To overcome and prosper from these uncertainties, IVCs need to minimize the effects of uncertainties. The significant uncertainties which exist for IVCs who invest in algae biodiesel are outlined in Chapters Five and Six.

The handbook is divided into the following chapters:

1. Microalgae Biodiesel Basics

2. Algae Challenges

3. Advantages of Algae Biodiesel

4. Disadvantages of Biodiesel from Algae

5. Algae Uncertainties

6. Macro Areas of Uncertainty in Investing

7. Best Practices Strategies

8. Future Investment in Algae

The references used for this handbook can be found at the end of the handbook, followed by a section which contains definitions of the various terms used in this report. The purpose of this handbook is to provide IVCs with the best practice strategies to reduce uncertainty when investing in algae biodiesel portfolio companies. IVCs who invest in biodiesel facilitate the process to provide a domestically secure, abundant, and sustainable energy source for the economy and contributing to cleaner and healthier communities throughout the United States.

CHAPTER 1

Microalgae Biodiesel Basics

The first step toward investing in algae biodiesel is to gain a basic understanding of algae. This chapter provides the IVC with information about what algae is and the relevance for the IVC who is considering investing in algae biodiesel companies. Because the production terminology of biodiesel fuel from algae tends to be technical, I have endeavored to make this chapter free of technical jargon for enhanced understanding of the topic.

Algae Basics

Humans have used algae for thousands of years for improved health, for nutrition, fuel, development of chemicals, cosmetics, and for medicinal purposes. Algae are microscopic, unicellular, photosynthetic chlorophyll-bearing plant-like organisms living in fresh and saltwater environments. The life forms are a primary source of food for many life forms on Earth. Algae requires CO_2, water, and sunlight to grow.

Algae convert sunlight, water, and carbon dioxide (CO_2) using photosynthesis to produce fifteen times more oil per day than other biofuel plants into biomass. Biomass is vegetation, plant material, or agricultural waste used as an energy source.

Algae develop in two forms: micro and macro. Microalgae are +/- 1 to 50ìm in size and macroalgae grow up to 60m in length. The focus of this handbook is on microalgae. Microalgae is important because the growth rate and yields are capable of producing more oil than other energy crops. Some estimates suggest that microalgae strains are capable of producing up to 50,000 liters of oil per hectare in one year. Algae biodiesel be used without modification to fuel vehicles from automobiles to airplanes. About 60% of algae's biomass can be converted into biofuel. The four main strains of algae are golden, diatoms, green, and blue-green.

Golden algae, usually referred to as chrysophytes, are a large group of algae primarily found in freshwater. Diatoms are unicellular photoplankton organisms and are able to live in both fresh and saltwater. Closely related to plants, green algae contains approximately 7000 different species. Green algae are unicellular and multi-cellular organisms growing in fresh and saltwater. The green algae group produces the vast majority of oil used in algae biodiesel. Finally, blue-green algae, also known as cynobacteria, obtain energy via photosynthesis and live in salt and freshwater.

As organizations in the United States require increasing levels of fuel because of expanding commercial markets, finding a sustainable source of energy is fundamental to continued economic, social, and environmental development. Biodiesel from algae may provide a solution to meet the transportation fuel needs for businesses that use petrol diesel in the United States.

The predominant source of fuel for transportation is petroleum derived from geopolitically unstable nations in the Middle East and in Latin America. Using petroleum from these areas contributes to national security concerns for the United States. Further, petroleum's combustion process is a source of greenhouse gases (GHG), which scientists believe might negatively affect the natural environment. Many environmental and national security concerns could be alleviated by businesses investing in large-scale, environmentally, socially and economically efficient, sustainable, nontoxic, biodegradable, and renewable biofuels.

Algae has been used as an energy feedstock since the 1950s. A feedstock is the raw materials required to make biodiesel. Generally, the selection of feedstock selection is based on considerations that will lower production costs, require less land use, and produce higher yields. Of all available biodiesel feedstock such as rapeseed, soybean, corn oil, waste vegetable oil, brassica juncea, canola, camelina, jatropha, seashore mallow, and animal fats; algae has the greatest potential to replace petrol diesel. The reasons why algae has the greatest potential to replace petrol diesel are outlined in this handbook.

A negative aspect of algae biodiesel use is during the 1980s and 1990s, the United States Department of Energy's Aquatic Species Program claimed biofuel production from algae provided relatively low oil yields. In addition, biofuel production might contribute to the contamination of native species, and be subject to high cultivating costs. However, uncertainty over future sources of petroleum has prompted researchers and businesses to locate scalable, biologically renewable sources of energy to augment or replace fossil fuels consumption. After the oil embargo against the United States in the 1970s, algae gained serious attention from business and science leaders. Starting in 1978 and concluding in 1998, the U.S. Department of Energy studied the use of algae as an energy source.

Without any modification to current systems, algae biodiesel can replace petrol. The process to convert algae oil into biodiesel is called transesterification. The challenge for algae oil producers is to achieve full-scale commercialization, high productivity, maximum biomass yields, and oil content while overcoming significant biotechnical, technological, and economic difficulties leading to economic uncertainties.

Although technological advances may lead to improved oil and biomass yields, technological advances alone will not be sufficient for algae to be priced competitively with petrol diesel.

Contemporary economies of scale need to improve to make algae fuel competitive with petrol diesel. In order to make the economies of scale more competitive, the high production and capital costs must be lowered, and a greater supply of algae feedstock made available. However, as the cost of extraction, refining, and distribution of petroleum continues to rise along with market speculation, depletion of fossil fuel reserves, and geopolitical considerations, algae biodiesel is becoming increaseingly attractive to consumers and investors.

CHAPTER 2

Algae Challenges

A multitude of technological challenges need to be addressed by entrepreneurial companies to develop a mature, and diverse algae biofuel sector. Among the challenges facing algae biodiesel use are production, engineering, ancillary issues, carbon neutrality, freshwater usage, degrees of uncertainty, photobioreactors, and open ponds.

Biofuel Production

The primary technical challenge in biofuel production is achieving yields making biofuels cost competitive with petroleum-based products. For any engineering approach to be successful, the development of efficient lignocellulosic (dry plant biomass) breakdown to monosaccharides is crucial. Monosaccharides are the basic form of a carbohydrate.

Scientists need to develop processes enabling the production of microalgae biodiesel with higher growth-rates, enhanced yields, lower soil-impacts, and less water use, fertilizer and pesticide requirements than are currently used in crops such as oil palms, corn, or soybeans. In order for algae biodiesel to have significant potential as a biofuel source, several issues must be addressed:

- Algae species selection balance requirements for biofuel production and extraction of valuable co-products,

- Attaining higher photosynthetic efficiencies through the continued development of production systems,

- Developing techniques for single species cultivation, evaporation reduction, and CO_2 diffusion losses,

- The potential for negative energy balance after accounting for requirements in water pumping, CO_2 transfer, harvesting, and extraction, and

- The incorporation of flue gases, which are unsuitable in high concentration owing to the presence of poisonous compounds such as nitrogen dioxide and sulfur dioxide.

In addition, he recovery of microalgae biomass

requires one or more solid liquid separation steps, meaning the algae biomass production process accounts for twenty to thirty percent of the total costs of production.

If the technical challenges are to be overcome, researchers must focus on nitrogen and phosphorus removal from wastewater using both physical and chemical methods. Each approach is costly and technically challenging.

Recent studies indicated microalgae has the potential for removing nitrogen and phosphorus from wastewater. These nutrients can be incorporated into algae cell biomass and subsequently removed from the wastewater. Algae treatment of wastewater, mediated through a combination of nutrient uptake, elevated pH, and dissolved oxygen concentration, can offer a more ecologically safer, cheaper, and more efficient means to remove nutrients and metals from wastewater than conventional tertiary treatment.

Commercial success with algae biodiesel has been limited despite decades of effort and significant research and development. One reason might be that high lipid algae, modified and grown in laboratory conditions, are very difficult to successfully transfer into mass culture systems. Another reason is the persistent challenge of simultaneously growing a sufficient quantity of biomass and maintaining high lipid productivity. Scientists suggest each reason is mutually exclusive and might be improbable to engineer in practice.

Algae are naturally adaptable to wide variations in aquatic and soil ecosystems, and can easily spread through abiotic (wind and rain) and biotic (plants and animals) processes. Like bacteria and yeast, eukaryotic algae and cyanobacteria have high generation rates and consequently have the potential to increase the extent of the genetic pool with an engineered trait through both genetic transfer and genetic adaptation. The genetic manipulation of algae to increase herbicide resistance, for example, is unlikely to have long-term sustainable benefits, as indigenous species have a high probability of rapidly acquiring this resistance.

Engineering

While the microbiological aspects of the harvesting process are extremely promising, the engineering aspects pose the greatest challenge. The main engineering problem is the cost of collection and harvesting. Algae grow as a thin surface layer on ponds, so harvesting miles and miles of growth to obtain large amounts of biodiesel is required. Huge ponds are required to grow microalgae in quantities that make the process commercially feasible.

Growing microalgae in natural lakes or ocean shores has been proposed. However, the invasiveness of algae could present an environmental hazard, since the grown algae will destroy and overtake the ecosystem. Nevertheless, a bounty of research funded by various US agencies exist. In addition, multinational oil companies such as Exxon and start-up biotechnology companies are attempting to make algae biodiesel a significant source of the diesel used in transportation over the next twenty to thirty years.

Weather

One of the challenges with algae biomass in the United States is year-round production. During the colder months, outdoor algae growing facilities and photobioreactors (PBRs) need to be controlled for optimum algae growth. Green house-based algae pro-duction may need heat from unsustainable sources to maintain high productivity. Greenhouses with solar panels to harvest solar energy or greenhouses to operate with the heat from geothermal could sub-stantially contribute to the sustainability issue. Indoor production capability would be particularly important in the future to contain GHG emissions.

Ancillary Issues

As the algae biofuel sector evolves into a mature industry, a myriad of ancillary and service based technologies such as algae monitoring devices and algae process control need to be developed for large scale commercial processing plants. Small business units and firms may play a role in the development of these ancillary industry needs. Key environmental policies are needed to facilitate a vibrant small bus-iness sector willing to take these innovations to market.

Carbon Neutrality

Carbon neutrality occurs as fuel usage does not add or reduce the amount of CO_2 emitted into the atmosphere. To achieve carbon neutrality, a defined set of technology breakthroughs will be required to develop for the optimum utilization of algae biomass for commercial production of biofuel. As no biofuel can be completely carbon neutral with current technology, significant fossil fuel input is needed for growing, processing, and extracting the oil, which might offset the positive aspects of the algae biofuel.

Freshwater Use

Algae biodiesel energy production using large amounts of freshwater competes with human needs. Globally, commercial bioenergy production is projected to consume 18% to 46% of the current water use by 2050. Already, the agricultural sector in the United States uses roughly 80% of the available freshwater and several regions face serious water shortages.

Degree of Uncertainty

A high degree of uncertainty exists in reducing the costs of extracting and harvesting algae for biodiesel purposes. The scalability and the sustainability in terms of natural resources use are continuing uncertainty concerns. The primary harvesting concern is the costs of PBRs and open ponds methods.

Photobioreactors

PBRs are best for single strain algae cultivation with little to no contamination. The advantages of PBRs are low contamination, continuous operation, controlled growth, high productivity, and efficient CO_2 capture. PBRs require little space, require less light and agricultural land, have lower cultivating costs than open ponds, but have high capital investment and operating costs. In addition, PBRs produce more algal broth than open ponds reducing costly dewatering issues.

Major concerns of PBRs are economic scalability challenges and technological design of producing cost effective biodiesel. The reasons are high capital investment costs, complex PBR designs, and scaling PBRs to produce large quantities of biodiesel.

Open ponds

Open pond systems are more widely used for cultivating algae than PBRs. The reasons are open pond systems have lower capital costs, are easier to operate, and can be built cheaper compared to PBRs. Capital costs can be reduced with further research and enhanced engineering design.

Estimates for the total capital cost for a 400 hectares open pond system would be $72,952 per hectare with operating costs (including debt service) of $30,658 per hectare. The capital costs for a typical PBR is $112,400 per hectare with operating costs of $39,300 per hectare. However, the capital costs are a significant uncertainty leading to even higher costs of producing algae biodiesel.

Regarding the algae oil to biodiesel production process, the total capital investment costs are estimated to be $10.9 million for 99.7% overall conversion of algae oil to biodiesel, and $10.5 million for ninety percent overall conversion of algae oil to biodiesel. The total direct equipment costs are estimated to be $2.6 million for the ninety percent overall algae oil to biodiesel conversion process and $2.8 million for the 99.7% overall conversion process. Ultimately the construction of larger, more efficient and better engineered open ponds over the next several years might lower capital costs.

Further Considerations

Uncertainties are significant considerations for IVC firms in deciding whether to invest in algae portfolio firms. Energy conversion, utilization and access underlie the profound challenges including those associated with sustainability, environmental quality, and security. Algae biofuels are an attractive alternative to current petroleum based fuels as they can be utilized as transportation fuels with little change to current technologies and have significant potential to improve sustainability and reduce GHG emissions.

Research on improving biofuel production has been accelerating for both ecological and economical reasons, primarily for its use as an alternative to petroleum based fuels. The most positive impact of biofuel is the reduction of GHGs emissions in production and consumption. The reason is biomass production utilizes atmospheric CO_2 and biomass is renewable.

On the other hand, mass production of biofuel can lead to the increase of GHG emissions by the utilization of fossil transportation fuels in the complicated logistics needed for biomass cultivation, collection, transportation and distribution of biofuel. The next two chapters explore the noteworthy advantages and disadvantages to help IVC firms to make better investment decisions.

CHAPTER 3

Advantages of Algae Biodiesel

Algae are the only source of biodiesel that can completely replace petrol diesel, and algae biodiesel is equivalent in performance to standard diesel. The use of algae for biodiesel production is environmentally friendly. The advantages of using algae as a source for biodiesel production are year-round growing cycles, high growth rates, noncompetition with food crops or human food supplies, positive environ-mental affects, is a versatile feedstock, greater volume yields, and broad product portfolio.

Year Round Growing

Algae can produce oil twenty-four hours a day every day of the year, replicating itself every three and one half hours to twenty-four hours. The growth cycle doubles in size every few days, which could provide a constant supply of energy. During the peak growth phase, some micro-algae can double every three and one-half hours. Year round growing is a distinct advantage for algae production. Algae are a potential prime source for biofuel because of higher biomass production, and greater photosynthetic efficiency compared to palm oil or jatropha.

High Growth Rates

Algae use photosynthesis to convert free sunlight into chemical energy. Having higher growth rates than any liquid substance, algae's yield per acre is seven to thirty-one times greater than palm oil, the closest competitor. Algae require forty-nine to 132 times less land area than other biodiesel feedstock's such as rapeseed or soybean crops. The dry weight oil content of algae could be as high as eighty percent.

Additionally, the rapid production cycle of algae biodiesel and high oil content ensures a stable supply. Algae contains no sulfur, are non-toxic, are biodegradable, and can be processed into ethanol. Algae oil is suitable to cold weather climates, and can reduce harmful emissions where grown.

Non-Compete with Food Crops

Because algae do not compete with human food crops such as corn and wheat, future food crises might not occur. For example, the global food crisis of 2007 to

2008 was caused in part due to the doubling of the price of corn and wheat. Corn and wheat allocated for food products went toward fuel production.

Algae feedstock does not require arable land to grow, can adapt to live in a variety of environmental conditions such as deserts, in salt, brackish, and fresh water unsuitable for plant or food production.

Because algae can grow in a multitude of environments, the use of the feedstock minimizes environmental impacts of freshwater use. Algae are best-suited to conform to the local environment or growth characteristics, which is not possible with other biodiesel feedstock such as palm oil, sunflower, rapeseed, or soybeans.

Positive Environmental Affects

Algae improves air quality by absorbing CO_2, a common industrial pollutant, from the atmosphere. By consuming CO_2, algae facilitates cell growth and produces oil. The cultivation of algae does not require pesticides or herbicides reducing the risk of polluting the atmosphere and waterways.

As a plant-like life form, algae are capable reducing CO_2 levels in the atmosphere. During photosynthesis, algae use solar energy to absorb CO_2 into biomass, so water used to cultivate algae must be enriched with CO_2. Algae offers an opportunity to make productive use of the CO_2 from power plants, biofuel facilities, and other sources. Algae poses no adverse effects on the ecosystem.

Versatile Feedstock

Algae are a feedstock for ethanol, methane, hydrogen, and biodiesel. Algae biodiesel performs as well as petrol diesel in transportation systems, while reducing carbon monoxide, CO_2, hydrocarbons, sulfur oxides, and emissions of particulate matter. Algae produces co-products such fertilizer, feed, methane, ethanol from the extracted oil. Varying algae growth conditions can change the biochemical composition of algae producing significantly en-hanced yields. Algae oil extracts are processed into ethanol and used for livestock feed.

Greater Volume Yields

Algae has the potential to yield greater volumes of biofuel per acre of production than other biofuel sources. Algae could yield more than 2,000 gallons of fuel per acre per year of production. Approximate yields for other fuel sources are much lower:

- Palm — 650 gallons per acre per year
- Sugar cane — 450 gallons per acre per year
- Corn — 250 gallons per acre per year
- Soybean — 50 gallons per acre per year

Broad Product Portfolio

The lipids produced by algae can be used to produce a wide range of biofuel, and the remaining biomass residue has a variety of useful applications similar to fossil fuels. Lipids can be used to generate heat, used in anaerobic digesters to produce methane, used as a fermentation feedstock in the production of ethanol, and used in value-added byproducts, such as animal feed.

Algae can be cultivated to produce a variety of products for large to small markets: plastics, chemical feedstock, lubricants, fertilizers, and even cosmetics. For many IVCs the value of algae is not in biodiesel but in the byproducts.

In summary, (a) algae grows fast, (b) has high biofuel yields, (c) absorbs CO_2, (d) does not compete with agriculture used for human food consumption, (e) the fuel produced works with current diesel technology without modification, (f) grows in almost any water source, and (g) can be used to create products to petroleum.

Future Considerations

Assuming the numerous technical challenges to achieving commercial-scale algae biofuel production can be met, adequate land and water are available to meet a significant portion of the U.S. renewable fuel goals. Locations in the Gulf Coast region are the most favorable in terms of land and freshwater demand.

Although additional land with relatively high production potential is available in the United States, accessibility of freshwater is likely to be a limiting factor. Moreover, the next step in assessing sustainable water resources availability is to consider current and future of competing fresh and saltwater requirements for other biofuels, agriculture, and thermoelectric cooling.

Clearly, the challenge facing algae oil commercialization is to achieve high productivity while reducing capital and operating costs. There are, however, a number of major technical challenges that will need to be overcome. Significant attention and support should be given to both basic and applied research on algae for biofuels applications and the engineering of sustainable microalgae systems. Algae productivity is the primary production cost determinant and so efforts should be focused on various aspects of algae that can have the greatest impact on growth rates and lipid biosynthesis.

CHAPTER 4

Disadvantages of Biodiesel from Algae

High production costs, inadequate scalability to meet market demand, lack of technological innovations, and government policy barriers are disadvantages of producing algae biodiesel. Estimates are that in ten to fifteen years, algae technological advances could transition algae biodiesel to full market scalability. The noteworthy disadvantages of manufacturing algae biodiesel are production issues, feedstock costs, technology advances, and engineering and biology challenges.

Production Issues

Estimates run that 0.53 billion m³ (cubic meter) of

biodiesel fuel would be required to replace U.S. petrol needs. The main constraint to the commercialization of algae biofuels is that algae are not cost competitive with other biofuels and petroleum. The four stages of algae biodiesel production are: cultivation, extraction, transesterification, and dewatering. Each stage requires high-energy use, which contributes to the overall high production costs. Cultivation costs are the most significant contributor to high production costs due to the large volume of algae cultures required to produce biodiesel.

Production Costs

The most significant costs in the production of algae biodiesel are feedstock costs. Feedstock costs are approximately seventy percent of the total operating costs for one gallon of algae biodiesel. In addition, cultivation systems, sales and administration costs, account for approximately twenty-three percent of the total production costs of producing algae biodiesel. The production cost per liter of algae biodiesel varies. Some estimate the cost per liter production cost from $0.48 per liter to $8.80 per liter. Generally, algae biodiesel production costs are two to three and a half times higher than petrol.

Feedstock Costs

Feedstock costs consist of raw materials, processing costs, and related expenses. Feedstock accounts for sixty to seventy-five percent of the total cost of producing biodiesel fuel in the United States. Harvesting costs add another twenty to twenty-five percent to the overall production costs from the use of centrifugation, filtration, sedimentation in the gravity field, and flotation. Selection of the harvesting method is dependent on the value of the algae products, size, and density. Estimates are that harvesting costs, which include capital and operating costs, as a percentage of total costs, account for forty to fifty percent of the twenty to twenty-five percent overall production costs. The reasons for the high cost are because of:

- Difficulty in optimal strain selection,

- Contamination management in open cultivation environments and in waste water/sewage,

- High capital and operating costs of photobioreactors,

- High cost of harvesting, and

- High cost of biomass gasification.

Technological Advances

The feasibility of reducing algae-based biofuels production costs to match petrol is dependent on technology. Noted British scientist, environmentalist, and futurologist James Lovelock postulated that a society needs approximately twenty-five years before a new major technological concept becomes fully accepted.

Reducing the cost of producing algae biodiesel and replacing petrol in the marketplace, requires innovative technological advances in developing low cost cultivating and harvesting processes, biorefinery based production strategies, engineering improvements in PBRs, and genetic engineering.

Regardless of technological and biological innovations, IVC investors look toward capital-intensive energy projects from an acceptable risk–return ratio perspective. To lower the production costs and increase the production of algae biodiesel requires an increase in optimal production conditions including light, CO_2, water, and mineral salts. The temperature in which algae are grown fluctuate between 20°C to 30°C.

In order to reduce biomass production costs, algae biodiesel production processes need to be based on readily available sunlight and an adequate supply of mineral elements such as nitrogen, phosphorus, iron, and silicon. Significant technological and economic challenges need to be overcome before algae can be a cost-effective meeting the global needs of transportation fuel consumers.

Engineering and Biology Challenges

Engineering challenges exist regarding photobio-reactors and open ponds. Biological concerns are focused on increasing oil yields, genetic engineering of algae strains, and facilitating specific strains of algae to survive in unnatural habitats.

Predicting when the biological challenges will be overcome is difficult. Scientific progress is being made on the genetic engineering of algae strains. If scientists are able to reduce cost, in the near future, algae biofuel may be an alternative energy source replacing fossil fuel use. Fossil fuel use has been attributed to the global warming phenomenon by releasing the GHG that might degrade the environment. Although significant challenges exist in investing in algae biodiesel, economic uncertainties might pose an even greater challenge for the IVC.

CHAPTER 5

Algae Uncertainties

The IVC must consider three significant algae uncertainty concerns: emission control schemes, capital costs, and cultivation costs. Emission control schemes are an external factor related to algae biodiesel as a process to reduce fossil fuels use in the economy. Reducing the potential affect of emission control schemes and finding solutions to lowering production and capital costs are critical in investing in algae.

Emission Control Schemes

Emission-restriction schemes such as cap and trade (C&T) also known as emissions trading could be implemented in the future. C&T is a market-based scheme to control GHG emissions where the government restricts the level of pollutants and sets a predetermined cap on emissions an organization can emit over a specified period, called a permit

Organizations that emit less than the cap can sell or trade permits to firms that have not reduced carbon emissions to preset levels. The concept is that the C &T scheme will reduce overall emissions while financially rewarding firms that have implemented efficient emission control systems.

Another emission scheme is the carbon tax where government assesses a tax on businesses that emit CO_2 and other fossil fuel pollutants. The purpose of the carbon tax is to remedy the negative externality costs in the form of added health care and environmental degradation costs not paid by the consumer in existing energy prices. Several states in the United States have considered assessing a carbon tax.

IVC Considerations

Under C&T, emission certainty exists with price and economic uncertainties, whereas with the carbon tax, emission uncertainty exists along with price and economic certainties. One result from implementing an emission control scheme is greater IVC investment in clean energy technologies. In order to implement emission control schemes, algae producers need to bring cost-effective algae biofuels products to market.

The uncertainty of the benefits and costs of mitigating GHG gases are important regarding uncertainties of algae. However, because of the uncertainty inherent in the debate regarding climate change and emission control schemes, organizations seeking to find renewable energy sources need to understand how economic-based emission control schemes shape climate mitigation efforts.

Capital Costs

Capital costs are a significant uncertainty. Primary capital costs for producing algae biodiesel are equipment purchase, building purchase, cultivation systems installation, and infrastructure. Standard deviation of capital costs among several studies is between $25 per liter and $72 per liter with a median of $4.30 per liter. The wide range of capital costs is related to the significant uncertainty related capital investment costs.

Annual capacity for plant-based ethanol capital investments production cost is from $1.06 to $1.48 per liter. Overall, capital costs are approximately forty percent of algae production costs. Construction of larger facilities and innovations in cultivation and harvesting technology over the next five years could lessen the uncertainty of algae capital costs. Capital investment costs for PBRs are ten times higher than for open pond systems.

Cultivation

Algae are cultivated in open ponds and PBRs. Cultivating costs are a major factor on algae strain selection affecting capital costs. Estimates of cultivating capital costs, as a percentage of total costs, vary considerably in different economic analyses because of economic uncertainty considerations.

The cultivation of algae makes up the largest proportion of energy use in the entire algae production process. No industry standards exist to account for the high energy, dewatering costs, and large-scale water use in algae biodiesel production. Because of a lack of cultivating standards, algae strain selection is a critical consideration in the cultivating process as specific algae species are less expensive to harvest than others. Greater energy efficiency, more cost-effective cultivating techniques, and better strain selection are critical to economic viability and might reduce economic uncertainty in producing algae oil.

CHAPTER 6

Macro Areas of Uncertainty in Investing

IVCs must be cognizant of the four areas of uncertainty when investing in algae biodiesel portfolio firms regardless of funding stage. The areas are technology, market, management, and government. The first uncertainty is technology.

Technology

IVCs must be willing to accept a moderate degree of uncertainty regarding the technology used by the biodiesel firm. Technological uncertainty can be ameliorated by lowering photobioreactor costs and incorporating genetic engineering innovations, which would reduce risk.

Market

IVCs must valuate market risk. How IVCs valuate market is risk debatable. Some IVCs perceive little uncertainty is prevalent in the market contingent upon competition existing for the portfolio firm's product. Other IVCs emphasize a need to understand market dynamics and predict consumer behavior. Others argue determining accurate sales predictions, market size, purchasing power of the market, targeting the correct market, and predicting market needs are critical uncertainties.

Most IVCs shun portfolio firms in niche or fringe markets. As part of the marketing mix, IVCs must insist portfolio firms have good products that meet the consumer's everyday needs. IVCs should demand a minimum of 3x revenue valuation, an executable marketing plan, and utilizing established relationship networks to increase market share before entering the portfolio firm into the market

Management

IVCs must have almost zero uncertainty related to algae energy technology and market knowledge of the portfolio management team. Portfolio firms must hire leaders with market and technology skills and industry expertise. Hiring qualified personnel in sales or other operational areas, sometimes with the assistance of IVCs, is essential for the success of the portfolio firm.

Government

The legislative process is a crucial uncertainty, especially related to algae biodiesel. As mentioned in Chapter Five, IVCs face legislative uncertainties from state and federal governments in terms of controlling GHG emissions. Other external factors IVCs must be cognizant of are new taxes on renewable energy products, and a reduction in subsidies provided by state and federal agencies to consumers. IVCs should seek to ameliorate governmental uncertainties by implementing best practices strategies.

CHAPTER 7

Best Practices Strategies

A best practice is the most effective, acknow-ledged, universal, repeatable, and efficient methods recommended by experts that facilitate an organization's achievement and implementation of a goal. The expected returns model and performing due diligence are two significant best practices stra-tegies IVCs must use when considering investing in algae biodiesel portfolio firms.

Expected Returns Model

Early stage renewable energy technology invest-ments exhibits higher levels of uncertainty than portfolio firms at an expansion stage or later stage. To alleviate high uncertainty, IVCs need effective best practices strategies. The purpose and goal of the IVC firm should be to create market value and to facilitate a successful exit through an IPO, merger, acquisition, or sale.

Early stage technology portfolio firms are often no more than a business plan or some notes on a napkin. Such firms have not commercialized products. Many early stage firm's business models are still developing, and management may not be seasoned or solidified. Often the portfolio firm has earned little revenue, or the technology is a prototype. Because early stage portfolio firms do not have a proven market space, investing in early stage firms provides the IVC with the greatest market and technology risks.

Effective business practice for IVC partners is to obtain higher expected returns while understanding that along with higher returns is an increased probability of failure because of asymmetric risk. To lessen asymmetric risk, partners can reduce uncertainty by using models such as multiples, net present value (NPV), and internal rate of return (IRR).

Multiples

Multiples are the primary returns model method used by IVCs. Using the expected returns model, IVCs intend to reduce uncertainty by calculating the valuation of the portfolio firm. Regardless of the investing stage, IVCs should demand at least multiples of 3x on revenue, 3x gross margin, or 3x net profit at exit. The recommended range of multiples is between 3x tand 10x based on investing stage and portfolio firm uncertainty.

IVC firms measure portfolio firm revenue while tracking the amount of funds raised from investors. Most venture capital funds exist for ten years and IVCs expect a successful exit within two to five years of initial funding.

Net Present Value (NPV)

NPV is the sum of the present value of a project's cash flows with the present values found by discounting all inflows and outflows at the project's cost of capital. If NPV is zero or higher, the project should be accepted, NPVs less than zero, should be rejected.

Note, a unique discount rate does not exist that will always be suitable for the calculation of NPV. In specific applications, the correct discount rate will often be a specified interest rate or rate of return. The formula for calculating NPV is:

$$NPV = -C_0 + \frac{C_1}{1+r} + \frac{C_2}{(1+r)^2} + ... + \frac{C_T}{(1+r)^T}$$

$-C_0 = Initial\ Investment$
$C = Cash\ Flow$
$r = Discount\ Rate$
$T = Time$

Internal Rate of Return (IRR)

IVCs use IRR to compare and measure the profitability of an investment by incorporating the time value of money. IRR is the discount rate equating the present value of a project's cash inflows to the present value of costs and outflows. For example, the following is an IRR estimation based on net cash flows (CF) for five years:

Initial Cost	-191000
Year 1 CF:	75000
Year 2 CF:	80000
Year 3 CF:	65000
Year 4 CF:	70000
Year 5 CF:	72000
IRR	26%

If the interest rate is less than the IRR, the project should be accepted.

Due Diligence

During the due diligence process, IVCs focus on reducing investment risk. Before making a financial investment, IVC firms perform extensive research on the portfolio firm's products, management team, legal actions, and internal and external competitive environments. Due diligence is measured by the total hours an IVC spends performing research on a portfolio company.

The effort spent by IVCs performing due

diligence is proportionate to the anticipated investment funding size. From screening to early funding stage can take approximately three to six months. Raising funds is time-consuming and difficult. IVC firms who conduct extensive due diligence and are involved in post investment operations of the portfolio firm experience significantly higher ROI through a successful exit. IVCs who focused on early funding opportunities experienced few negative exits.

IVCs perform due diligence to reduce uncertainty in early stage investments. The most significant due diligence process is the use of comparables from online venture capital databases. The databases are used to determine valuation price and evaluate similar portfolio firms in the market before deciding to invest. If not knowledgeable, IVCs should consult with market experts to understand market trends and requirements.

Considering market trends, IVCs target portfolio firm valuation should be priced three to five years into the future. IVCs should consider whether the portfolio firm has a scalable technology, a market need for the technology, and that the technology can solve an everyday need. Due diligence is needed to evaluate revenue uncertainty. For most IVCs, revenue supersedes the use any model.

As part of the due diligence process, IVCs need to predict whether the portfolio company can be financially sustainable within three years. Qualitative factors IVCs should consider include the use of 'gut feelings' related to investing in the portfolio firm.

IVCs should have good personal chemistry with the portfolio management team. The IVC must be confident the portfolio firm management understands industry standards and demands. Most importantly, IVCs should use qualitative and quantitative factors to determine how much time (three to five years) and money (ten million, fifty million, one hundred million) are needed to achieve a successful exit.

IVC must remain dispassionate at all times so not to lose objectivity of achieving a high return on investment. The due diligence period is usually between six and eight weeks. As part of the due diligence process, IVCs might consider the use an 180-day plan scaled from one to five to assess risk and provide time to determine any changes in the technology, the management team, government action, or market conditions.

CHAPTER 8

Future Investment in Algae

With oil prices over $100 per barrel and rising, creating a secure domestic source of renewable energy is critical for the economic security of the United States. By 2020, estimates of algae biofuel production will reach sixty-one million gallons per year, command a market value of $1.3 billion, and have an annual growth rate of seventy-two percent. When the price of a gallon of algae biodiesel is competitive with petrol diesel, IVC industry investment and production output will likely increase.

The U.S. military has been actively exploring ways to reduce the annual $14 billion dollar fuel bill. The Department of Defense has spent over $2.7 billion dollars to improve energy efficiency. An army study found that for every twenty-four fuel convoys, one soldier or marine is killed. By 2020, fifty percent of the U.S. Navy and Marines' power will be supplied by renewable sources. The Army and Air Force are also developing biofuels for vehicles and aircraft.

Other countries than the United States are betting on algae as well. Intense interest in algae biofuels and bioproducts come from Australia, Chile, China, the European Union, Japan, Korea, New Zealand, Israel, and others. The Asia Pacific region has been culturing algae for food and pharmaceuticals for many centuries.

Biofuel investors and scientists agree that several more years of sustained research, development and demonstration will be necessary to overcome the cost and scale barriers associated with algae biofuels. In the meantime, first movers will push the industry closer to realizing the full potential of algae biodiesel technology by producing meaningful quantities of fuels and products.

The significant issue for the algae biodiesel industry is to develop cheaper more effective technologies to convert algae into biofuels. The costs vary depending on the economic environment and method used to extract oil, but as it stands now, conservative estimates place the retail price of algae oil at $8 per gallon. Reducing the price will require streamlining technology, expanding pilot projects to increase yield, and producing more profitable co-products like chemicals, plastics, lubricants, beauty and pharmaceutical items.

Without sustained high fuel prices at the pump, investment in algae will likely be driven by demand for other products. In the short term, the growth of the algae industry will come from governments and companies seeking to reduce environmental impacts through carbon remediation. The challenge in the application of microalgae for commercial purposes is to focus only on products with a large market and or profit potential where the use of microalgae leads to clear competitive advantage. Fuel and food offer the largest algae markets.

The growth of microalgae to solve the world food shortage has in the past been considered, but the wide scale commercial growth of algae for human food is restricted mainly to health foods, food supplements, and food additives. The health food market is the branch of algae production with the highest sales, but the market is dependent on a number of claims of health benefits without the necessary scientific proof of efficacy.

Concluding Thoughts

The purpose of this handbook was to provide IVCs will basic knowledge of algae and best practices strategies when investing in algae biodiesel. The handbook should be used as a quick reference guide and does not provide in-depth analysis. The handbook is not a substitute for IVCs using his or her knowledge, experience, and analysis before investing in an algae producing portfolio firm.

IVCs must be cautious and aware of uncertainties inherent in investing in algae biodiesel. Understanding the advantages and challenges in implementing best practice strategies can reduce the uncertainties of investing in algae biodiesel.

The significant benefit of algae biodiesel is algae biodiesel produces low emissions and is renewable sourced. A noteworthy consideration is algae diesel can run in current diesel engines and will lubricate engines, cutting down on wear an tear. Most significantly, algae biodiesel contributes toward decreasing the United States dependency on foreign sources of oil. Algae are the quickest growing plants in the world, producing thirty times more energy per acre than any other biofuel source. Algae do not need valuable land to grow. Algae can be produced in fresh water, saltwater, and contaminated water.

The significant challenge is algae biodiesel is uncompetitively priced with petrol diesel. Some reasons for the price differentials were mentioned in this handbook. Technology, market, and government uncertainties are relevant for investing in algae biodiesel. While the IVC has a measure of control to reduce technology and market uncertainty, the IVC is harder pressed to control legislative uncertainty.

One issue with government policy makers is the assessment fees on consumers to capture the negative externality costs associated with fossil fuel use. Externality costs are costs not captured in the manufacturing process. The use of petrol today is similar to the use of stones by ancient humans. The

Stone Age did not end because humans ran out of stones, rather, the Stone Age ended because the externality costs associated with the Stone Age were too high.

In the same way today, the externality costs associated with fossil fuel use will force industry to seek sustainable forms of fuel energy. If externality costs were added to a gallon of petrol, rather than paying $4.00 a gallon, the consumer might pay $10.00 per gallon. Although algae biodiesel has many challenges and even more advantages, the IVC should seriously consider investing in algae biodiesel portfolio firms.

REFERENCES

Brennan, L., & Owende, P. (2010). Biofuels from microalgae—A review of technologies for production, processing, and extractions of biofuels and co-products. *Renewable and Sustainable Energy Reviews, 14*, 557-577. doi:10.1016/j.rser.2009.10.009

Campbell, P. K., Beer, T., & Batten, D. (2011). Life cycle assessment of biodiesel production from microalgae in ponds. *Bioresource Technology, 102*, 50-56. doi:10.1016/j.biortech.2010.06.048

Carriquiry, M. A., Du, X., & Timilsina, G. R. (2011). Second generation biofuels: Economics and policies. *Energy Policy, 39*, 4222-4234. doi:10.1016/j.enpol.2011.04.036

Chen, P., Min, S. M., Chen, Y., Wang, L., Li, Y., Chen, Q., ... Ruan, R. (2009). Review of the biological and engineering aspects of algae to fuels approach. *International Journal of Agricultural and Biological Engineering, 2*, 1-30. doi:10.3965/j.issn.l934-6344.2009.04.001-030

Cheng, C.-T., Lo, S.-L., & Lin, T. T. (2011). Applying real options analysis to assess cleaner energy development strategies. *Energy Policy, 39*, 5929-5938. doi:10.1016/j.enpol.2011.06.048

Chisti, Y., & Yan, J. (2011). Energy from algae: Current status and future trends: Algal biofuels – A status report. *Applied Energy, 88*, 3277-3279. doi:10.1016/j.apenergy.2011.04.038

Cooney, M. J., Young, G., & Pate, R. (2011). Bio-oil from photosynthetic microalgae: Case study. *Bioresource Technology, 102*, 166-177. doi:10.1016/j.biortech.2010.06.134

Demirbas, A., & Demirbas, A. F. (2011). Importance of algae oil as a source of biodiesel. *Energy Conversion and Management, 52*, 163-170. doi:10.1016/j.enconman.2010.06.055

Ford, S. J., Mortara, L., & Probert, D. R. (2012). Disentangling the Complexity of Early-Stage Technology Acquisitions. *Research-Technology Management, 55*(3), 40-48 doi:10.5437/08956308X550304

Gallagher, B. J. (2011). The economics of producing biodiesel from algae. *Renewable Energy, 36*, 158-162. doi:10.1016/j.renene.2010.06.016

Harun, R., Davidson, M., Doyle, M., Gopiraj, R., Danquah, M., & Forde, G. (2011). Technoeconomic analysis of an integrated microalgae photobioreactor, biodiesel and biogas production facility. *Biomass and Bioenergy, 35*, 741-747. doi:10.1016/j.biombioe.2010.10.007

He, Y., Wang, L., & Wang, J. (2012). Cap-and-trade vs. carbon taxes: A quantitative comparison from a generation expansion planning perspective. Computers & Industrial Engineering, *63*, 708-716. doi:10.1016/j.cie.2011.10.005

Huang, G., Chen, F., Wei, D., Zhang, X., & Chen, G. (2010). Biodiesel production by microalgal biotechnology. *Applied Energy, 87*, 38-46. doi:10.1016/j.apenergy.2009.06.016

Jakóbiec, J., & Wądrzyk, M. (2010). Microalgae as a potential source for biodiesel production. *Agricultural Engineering, 6*(124), 51-56. Retrieved from http://ir.ptir.org/index.php?mood=article&article_id=2846&language=en

John, R. P., Anisha, G. S., Nampoothiri, K. N., & Pandey, A. (2011). Micro and macroalgal biomass: A renewable source for bioethanol. *Bioresource Technology, 102, 186-193.* doi:10.1016/j.biortech.2010.06.139 , 6(124),

Johnson, M. B. & Wen, Z. (2010). Development of an attached microalgal growth system for biofuel production. *Applied Microbiology and Biotechnology, 85*, 525-534. doi:10.1007/s00253-009-2133-2

Kovacevic, V., & Wesseler, J. (2010). Cost-effectiveness analysis of algae energy production in the EU. *Energy Policy, 38*, 5749-5757. doi:10.1016/j.enpol.2010.05.025

Lardon, L., Elias, A., Sialve, B., Steyer, P., & Bernard, O. (2009). Life-cycle assessment of biodiesel production from microalgae. *Environmental Science & Technology, 43*, 6475-6481. doi:10.1021/es900705j

Lee, D. H. (2011). Algal biodiesel economy and competition among bio-fuels. *Bioresource Technology 102*, 43-49. doi:10.1016/j.biortech.2010.06.034

Lehtonen, O., & Lahti, T. (2009). The role of advisors in the venture capital investment process. *Venture Capital an International Journal of Entrepreneurial Finance, 11*, 229-254. doi:10.1080/13691060902972851

Li, Y. (2008). Duration analysis of venture capital staging: A real options perspective. *Journal of Business Venturing, 23*, 497-512. doi:10.1016/j.jbusvent.2007.10.004

Li, Y., & Mahoney, J. T. (2011). When are venture capital projects initiated? *Journal of Business Venturing, 26*, 239-254. doi:10.1016/j.jbusvent.2009.08.001

Li, Y., & Zahra, S. A. (2012). Formal institutions, culture, and venture capital activity: A cross-country analysis. *Journal of Business Venturing, 27*, 95-111. doi:10.1016/j.jbusvent.2010.06.003

Mata, T. M., Martins, A. A., & Caetano, N. S. (2010).
     Microalgae for biodiesel production and other
     applications: A review. *Renewable and
     Sustainable Energy Reviews, 14,* 217-232.
     doi:10.1016/j.rser.2009.07.020

Matusik, S. F., & Fitza, M. A. (2012). Diversification in
     the venture capital industry: Leveraging
     knowledge under uncertainty. *Strategic
     Management Journal, 33,* 407-426. doi:
     10.1002/smj.1942

Milledge, J. J. (2010). Commercial application of
     microalgae other than as biofuels: A brief
     review. *Reviews in Environmental Science and
     Biotechnology, 10,* 31-41.
     doi:10.1007/s11157-010-9214-7

Mutanda, T., Ramesh, D., Karthikeyan, S., Kumari, S.,
     Anandraj, A., & Bux, F. (2011). Bioprospecting
     for hyper-lipid producing microalgal strains
     for sustainable biofuel production.
     Bioresource Technology, 102, 57-70.
     doi:10.1016/j.biortech.2010.06.077

Oltra, C. (2011). Stakeholder perceptions of biofuels
     from microalgae. *Energy Policy, 39,* 1774-
     1781. doi:10.1016/j.enpol.2011.01.009

Percoco, P., & Borgonovo, E. (2012). A note on the
     sensitivity analysis of the internal rate of
     return. *International Journal of Production
     Economics, 135,* 526-529.
     doi:10.1016/j.ijpe.2011.09.002

Pienkos, P. T., & Darzins, A. (2009). The promise and
     challenges of microalgal-derived biofuels

Biofuels, Bioproducts, & Biorefining, 3, 431-440. doi:10.1002/bbb.159

Richardson, J. W., Johnson, M. D., & Outlaw, J. L. (2012). Economic comparison of open pond raceways to photo bio-reactors for profitable production of algae for transportation fuels in the Southwest. *Algal Research, 1*, 93-100. doi:10.1016/j.algal.2012.04.001

Singh, A., Nigam, P. S., & Murphy, J. D. (2011). Renewable fuels from algae: An answer to debatable land based fuels. *Bioresource Technology, 102*, 10-16. doi:10.1016/j.biortech.2010.06.032

Strömsten, T., & Waluszewski, A. (2012). Governance and resource interaction in networks. The role of venture capital in a biotech start-up. *Journal of Business Research, 65*, 232-244. doi:10.1016/j.jbusres.2010.11.030

Weitzman, M. L. (2009). On modeling and interpreting the economics of catastrophic climate change. *The Review of Economics and Statistics, 91*, 1-19. doi:10.1162/rest.91.1.1

Wilkie, A. C., Edmundson, S. J., & Duncan, J. G. (2011). Indigenous algae for local bioresource production: Phycoprospecting. *Energy for Sustainable Development, 15*, 365-371. doi:10.1016/j.esd.2011.07.010

Williams, P. J. L., & Laurens, L. M. L. (2010). Microalgae as biodiesel & biomass feedstocks: Review & analysis of the biochemistry, energetics & economics. *Energy &*

Environmental Science, 3, 554-590.
doi:10.1039/b924978h

Wiltbank, R., Read, S., Dew, N., & Sarasvathy, S. D.
(2009). Prediction and control under
uncertainty: Outcomes in angel investing.
Journal of Business Venturing, 24, 116-133.
doi:10.1016/j.jbusvent.2007.11.004

Wonglimpiyarat, J. (2009). The influence of capital
market laws and initial public offering (IPO)
process on venture capital. *European Journal
of Operational Research, 192*, 293-301.
doi:10.1016/j.ejor.2007.09.007

Yung, C. (2009). Entrepreneurial financing and costly
due diligence. *The Financial Review, 44*, 137-
149. doi:10.1111/j.1540-6288.2008.00213.x

Zamalloa, C., Vulsteke, E., Albrecht, J., & Verstraete, W.
(2011). The techno-economic potential of
renewable energy through the anaerobic
digestion of microalgae. *Bioresource
Technology, 102*, 1149-1158.
doi:10.1016/j.biortech.2010.09.017

Zhang, J. (2011). The advantage of experienced start-
up founders in venture capital acquisition:
Evidence from serial entrepreneurs. *Small
Business Economic, 36*, 187-208.
doi:10.1007/s11187-009-9216-4

Zhu, L. (2012). A simulation based real options
approach for the investment evaluation of
nuclear power. *Computers & Industrial
Engineering, 63*, 585-593.
doi:10.1016/j.cie.2012.02.012

DEFINITION OF TERMS

Algae: Microscopic, unicellular, photosynthetic, aquatic, relatively simple organisms living in fresh and saltwater environments that convert sunlight, water, and carbon dioxide into biomass.

Best practices: Effective, acknowledged, universal, repeatable, and efficient methods recommended by experts that facilitate organizations' achievement and implementation of a goal.

Biodiesel: Gasoline produced by combining animal, vegetable, or algae oils with an alcohol to produce diesel fuel.

Biomass: Vegetation, plant material, or agricultural waste used as an energy source to make biodiesel.

Cap and trade: Market-based scheme to control greenhouse gas emissions whereby the government restricts the level of pollutants and sets a predetermined cap on emissions an organization can emit over a specified period called a permit.

Carbon tax: Governmental policy to assess a tax on businesses that emit carbon dioxide and other fossil fuel pollutants.

Independent venture capitalist (IVC): Individual who raises funds from institutional and high net worth investors and invest funds in an entrepreneurial-based portfolio company with expected high returns created from a successful exit strategy.

Internal rate of return (IRR): Capital budgeting tool based on net present value used to determine the rate of return an investor expects from an investment expressed as a percentage.

Net present value (NPV): Summation of every future cash flow during a specific period of an investment.

Photobioreactor (PBR): Vertical column, flat-plate, and tubular designed systems where algae are cultivated.

Portfolio firm: Organization receiving IVC investment funding.

Uncertainty: Lack of information in the external environment where the randomness of multiple outcomes is not influenced by individual organizations.

ABOUT THE AUTHOR

David A. Blum holds a Doctor of Business Administration and a Master of Business Administration in Sustainable Business. Dr. Blum's research interests include financial viability of investing in liquid renewable energy fuels such as algae biodiesel, reducing macroeconomic uncertainty in venture capital investing, gender disparity in venture capital management, strategies to increase success ratio of venture capital exists, and valuation of capital budgeting investment projects using real options theory. Dr. Blum is the co-author of *Real Life Real Investing and How to Collect Rent: Adventures in Property Management.*

www.ingramcontent.com/pod-product-compliance
Lightning Source LLC
Chambersburg PA
CBHW070826210326
41520CB00011B/2126